Beach in City Island

Haiku Poems by David Ellis

Design by MRFA Designs

First Printing, 2016

ISBN: 978-0-578-18875-1

Dedicated to my son Gabriel,
may you always have a shell
in your pocket and
sand between your toes.

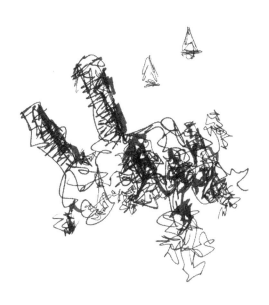

Contents

Contents

Contents

The sun will come out

Waiting for the rain   to stop

I know it will

Beautiful Morning

Feeling the sun on my face

Autumn lapping waves

Sleeping just like us

The dark clouds surround the moon

Calm and just peaceful

I'm a black ocean

Sun warms my soul in the day

Moon makes my heart dance

Sun baked summer days

Getting shorter   everyday

I can taste autumn

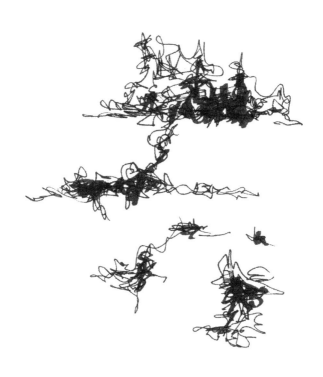

Felt the wind on me

Watched the thick clouds
                   change colors

Heard the cicada

Sun stretches its legs

    Just the sound of lapping waves

Watching seagulls play

No more dark grey clouds

He returned just like the sun

Even the bees smiled

The rainbow will come

    Don't run away from your heart

And also the sun

Birds create their nest

Sun dances on the water

Tranquil spring morning

Day without the sun

Sky and water is steel gray

Rain on windowpane

God in all of us

Shining even in the dark

All of us are one

Flock of birds fly high

The sun begins to relent

Ruby gold sunset

Air is crisp and sweet

The sun melts away slowly

Can see sand again

They searched the ocean

It was inside
their hearts

But they did not know

Endless summer days

They're slowly fading away

Splash of evening waves

Sun shines
          moon is clear

Our footprints still in sand

        Seagulls soar in air

Charcoal sky morning

Disappearing   in the clouds

Raindrops on my cheek

Refusing to leave

Seagull pacing back
and
forth

Watching me on beach

Seagull glides away

A burst of sun on my face

Watching the kids play

Days of sea and sun

Feeling free like the seagulls

Horseshoe crabs are back

Sun shines on water

Green leaves sprout
                    on tree branches

Seagulls squawk birds chirp

Soaring above the clouds

Love you so much that it hurts

Smile bright as the sun

The ocean has eyes

As the waves come in slowly

Watching us closely

Flock of birds in sky

All turning at the same time

Golden blue sunrise

Ripples on water

The seagulls fly together

Beautiful morning

The sun comes and goes

Finding freedom   in the sea

As dogs play on beach

Gods lamp at night

As we watch the sun's shadow

Beautiful and bright

Seagull on the rocks

Flying away as I walk

        Closer to see her

The tides coming in

Look up here
　　　　　I'm in heaven

Sand covers my feet

Waiting for low tide

Walking on the sand barefoot

Stepping over snails

All of us are one

Souls lay bare like our feet

On the sand and rocks

The blue water danced

At peace
        with the rising sun

Geese flying above

Sun waves sand and birds

Flowing all over my soul

All in unison

I hope that it snows

Wonder if the seagulls know

That it is Christmas

Waiting for low tide

Up early before sunrise

Grey bucket in hand

High tide turning low

Ladybug played with the kids

Not a cloud in sight

As time passes on

Moments to last a lifetime

Always in my heart

White just like the snow

Cold morning as the waves roar

Glad your sweater's on

Licking our boots

Seagulls return when you leave

Running free on beach

Snow finally arrived

    Most melted by the night

We had a good time

Alone in the night

Water is black like the sky

Beautiful feathers

Heading back to beach

It's just us and the seagulls

Watching you kick leaves

Brighter than before

I've become an orange moon

    Reflecting   your light

Pure fluctuation

At peace with the rising sun

Body   mind   and soul

It is the people

Everyday of the season

Who are the treasure

Barely spoke english

We still communicated

The beach translated

Haven for Spirits

Where everyone   comes to play

The young and the old

Invited their friends

The seagulls joined us for lunch

And their family

In all of the storms

Still like the rocks that I watch

Not moving at all

Seagulls glide in air

The windmill is spinning fast

Waves crashing so loud

Under the half moon

Wonder if it can hear you

As you laugh so loud

Dont stop believing

I will forever love you

The power of now

Heart beats like the waves

Worshiping by the water

Surrounded by God

Didnt stay for long

Will be in their hearts always

Sweet sounds from the birds

Morning sun warms us

Only the heron is up

Pacing slow for food

Sebastian! He shouts

The old man with his two dogs

On early mornings

Running on the sand

So young playing together

They dont even know

Nourishing the soul

Awareness in the moment

Swelling and   churning

Morning rain 5 ducks

Afternoon evening sun hides

Stars   in the night sky

Holes in the driftwood

Waves roaring like a lion

Taste it on my lips

Miss you sweet August

Wake me when September ends

Stomach feels nauseous

Sun shines on water

Waves come in steady and strong

I'm still like the rocks

Gorgeous afternoon

Waves pound themselves into foam

Seagulls search for food

Heron pacing slow

Low tide birds fly over you

Standing immobile

Just the birds chirping

Perfect tranquility reigns

Waiting for the sun

Holding on to you

    July feels so good on me

I can't let you go

Sail out of your head

    Enjoy each and every wave

Paddling with your soul

Clouds are still dreaming

Sun beginning to wake up

The waves are snoring

A new day brings hope

Like a rainbow in the sky

Yesterday is gone

Lifting off the trees

Cant see the water or sun

Feel and hear them both

Hearing the soft waves

Blessed to see another day

Your smile   and your face

Golden sand and sun

Feeling free
        like the seagulls

Glad you're here with me

Born to die like us

So many scattered on sand

Covered in seaweed

Splashing in water

Feet in the air not a care

Sun belongs to them

Clear deep sapphire

Constant current keep flowing

Don't become stagnant

Birds flapping their wings

Children laughing in the spring

Waves are coming in

Beach is your playground

Hermit crabs and sand castles

Sea glass and sea shells

The night you were born

Waves were gentle
                 just like you

The stars shined so bright

45020107R00060

Made in the USA
Middletown, DE
22 June 2017